1981

WEALTH OF THE MIND

Wealth of the Mind

by

ERNA E. WISSMANN

PHILOSOPHICAL LIBRARY
New York

Copyright, 1971, by PHILOSOPHICAL LIBRARY, INC.,
15 East 40 Street, New York, New York 10013
All rights reserved

Library of Congress Catalog Card No. 70-137788
SBN 8022-2047-9

Manufactured in the United States of America

Table of Contents

Preface

FRUITS OF RIGHT THINKING

Sometimes life seems to present a series of challenges and you may think that you have more than your share of problems. Is there a way to meet these challenges without being overwhelmed? The answer is YES, and this book was written with the express purpose in mind of trying to help people live with less strain and tension in today's world.

You have the power to bring great blessings into your life. You have the power to judge, plan, and direct your course. It is one thing to know this, another to do it. Jesus said, "If ye know these things, happy are ye if ye do them." John 13:17.

Since you are always thinking, why not use the tremendous power you are constantly exerting in a constructive way? Some times people say, "it sounds good, but does it really work?" Well, the only way to find out is to put it to the test.

Just remember that years of wrong thinking are not changed in five minutes. It requires effort, concentration, and a willingness to work consistently with a new idea, so that it can take hold, but the rewards are worth the effort. You have to make a start sometime, why not Now?

The subconscious mind is a great treasure storehouse. We all need to appreciate the wonders of the mind. It asks only respect and recognition. The God-mind within is always at work caring for the body, and for our wellbeing. The Divine Mind awaits acceptance so that it may bring us to the pinnacle of spiritual understanding, that the glories of the heaven within us may be extended to the earth.

Being a minister, I have had many people come to me with their problems. I have had the joyous opportunity of seeing disillusioned, unhappy people gain peace of mind, make new beginnings, achieve prosperity, and harmonize home conditions by applying the principles of right think-ing and appreciating the treasures in the subconscious mind.

You are important. You have the power to consciously direct your thinking, so that your life will be glorious. As you read the true experiences of people who have been helped through the science of mind, you will understand that you are not the only person who has suffered disap-pointment and heartache, but that many of your fellow men have had similar experiences and have risen above them. If you are bewildered or beset with difficulties, learn to call upon the power of Divine Mind in a scientific way to dissolve your difficulties. "They that sow in tears shall reap in joy." Psalm 126:5.

Begin to see beauty and goodness everywhere and add a new dimension to living.

ERNA E. WISSMANN

WEALTH OF THE MIND

CHAPTER 1

The Law Works

Let us begin an adventure in learning how the law of mind really works. We will open the Bible and see what we can learn about the power of mind. There is a clue to the way in which the subconscious mind works in Malachi 3:1. "Behold I will send my messenger, and he shall prepare the way before me.**" When we hand over an idea to the subconscious mind it goes about its work in an orderly manner to prepare the groundwork for the development of the idea. The first thing the subconscious does, is to send out a messenger or "feeler" to make sure it is moving in the right direction.

The mind has great powers of selectivity. The more familiar it is with a subject, the sooner it can bring back information through the thought messengers. When it explores unfamiliar territory it takes longer. It must feel its way along an unknown terrain and proceed cautiously until it gains a foot-hold. It is like an explorer viewing new territory. He must become familiar with it. This is also shown in the story of Moses as he prepared for the conquest of the land of Canaan. He sent out spies and said to them "and see the land, what it is."

Before starting upon a new venture that requires the investment of talents, time and money, it is well to "see the land. Do not observe only the favorable aspects, but ferret

1

out the weak spots as well. This is necessary to the success of any venture.

When Moses' spies returned they reported that Canaan was a land that flowed with milk and honey; the soil was rich and they brought back grapes, pomegranates, and figs to prove it. However, they stated that it would be difficult to conquer. The Canaanites were strong, in fact they reported that they were giants. The spies thought of themselves as grasshoppers and considered the risk too great.

Among those that Moses had sent out, were two men of faith and courage, Joshua and Caleb. They tried to allay the fears of the people and reminded them that the land could be conquered. They assured them it was worth conquering, but it would take courageous measures. However, fear was deep-seated in the children of Israel and they turned against Joshua and Caleb. These men were nevertheless dauntless; they kept the dream alive in their hearts and minds and nurtured it with faith. Eventually they realized the fulfillment of their goals while the grumblers died in the wilderness.

If you believe that your goal can be attained, that it is not an impossible one, but you find obstacles in the way, endeavor to overcome the stumbling blocks. Often fear comes to the surface and at such a critical time it is easy to quit. When the children of Israel learned that it would take hard work and sacrifice to conquer Canaan they wept and found fault with Moses.

The science of mind teaches you how to overcome your fears and reminds you that the law always works. Clear thinking is imperative to success. It enables you to realize your dreams, achieve your goals, and prosper in your undertakings.

Fears are not man's only handicaps. Impatience is also a deterrent. The impatient person becomes irritable when things do not move quickly enough to satisfy him. He frequently disregards the promptings of Divine Mind and en-counters difficulties. When he is beset with troubles of his own making he is disgruntled, and remains oblivious of the fact that worthwhile goals are achieved only after years of patient, loving labor and effort.

Suppose you want to start a new business. If so, consider your skills and aptitudes, also, whether you have sufficient capital to tide you over until the business is firmly estab-lished. Many a person has started a business on faith, but be sure your faith is strong enough to carry you through. Jesus gave some sound advice on the subject. He said, "For which of you, desiring to build a tower, does not first sit down and count the cost, whether he has enough to com-plete it?" Luke 14:28. When you have sufficient facts then you are ready to decide upon a course of action. Once a decision is reached, have faith and carry through. The out-come will be good.

A director of a building and loan association told me how he started on his way to prosperity. He had built every house on one of the streets in his community. He said proudly, "I built substantial homes and never over-reached, nor did I attempt to go beyond my means and in that way I was not burdened mentally with the thought of debt. I never worried if a house did not sell immediately because I always saw my way clear to meet my obligations and never allowed anyone to talk me into taking on more than I could handle. Today, I have no financial worries, and at an age when most people are retired, I am still active in business." He retired at the age of eighty-nine.

Perhaps you have been working for a long time for a promotion or recognition in your field of service, or for a greater income, but instead of moving forward, you find your moorings torn away, and you seem to be drifting farther and farther away from the goal you are seeking. That is the time to hold on, have faith, and also some self-

3

examination to see if you are pursuing the right course. There are times when Divine Mind seems to move us from one place or condition to another in order to fulfill its purpose, and in this process there may be a feeling of defeat and discouragement. Actually you may be making more progress than you dream of, so be ready for the greater opportunity when it appears.

The law of mind always works from the inner to the outer. It weighs, ponders and considers, and if given enough time, comes up with the right answer. Many problems are caused because too much is attempted too soon, or the subconscious is given a directive and then it is countermanded. The man who teeters and seesaws cannot make up his mind and therefore does not arrive at satisfactory conclusions. Big projects require the assumption of responsibilities, and therefore should not be undertaken unless you want to assume them.

The inner wisdom has a perfect sense of timing. Do not feel thwarted because straws in the winds are not immediately evident. At the right time every thing falls into place.

The question is often asked, "How can I recognize the right answer?" There is a definite feeling, an assurance, when it comes through. Often it is not a question of knowing or recognizing the right answer. It may be rejected because of its requirements. If there are certain requirements for the success of an enterprise they must be fulfilled.

A woman who had been studying painting for a short time entered her pictures in an exhibit and they were not accepted by the judges. She became very angry, scolded one of the judges, sulked and pouted. She complained to a good friend and received quite a jolt. Instead of sympathizing with her, the friend told her that she was unfair and conceited. She went on to say that the paintings that had been accepted were those of people who had studied and painted for years. They had earned their places in the ex-

4

hibit. She argued but her friend refused to budge from her position and reminded the amateur painter that she knew very little about the art of painting.

The woman went home and thought over the situation. She prayed for understanding and came to the realization that her friend was right. First, she telephoned the judge she had berated and apologized, and then set herself to the task of studying and working diligently. A few years later her pictures showed real progress and she was invited to exhibit. This time her pictures were accepted and, because she had learned a lesson in humility, she was rewarded. She sold most of the pictures before the exhibit was over.

If you trust your life to God you must be willing to change your mind, and follow divine guidance.

A poised and happy woman told me that she had learned early in life to accept with good graces whatever situation she had to face. With her children in grade school, she found it advisable to secure a position to augment the family income. She had planned to teach school but there was no opening at the time in the small town in which they lived. She then took a part-time office position which developed into a full time position and eventually she became an executive in the manufacturing firm where she was employed.

No time was spent regretting her inability to obtain a teaching position, but she gave her best to the work that was offered to her. She listened to the guidance of Divine Mind and followed its leadings.

Attempts to force prosperity or success only spell trouble.

A family faced with a foreclosure suit and the possible loss of their home came to me with their problem. The husband was a business man who headed a small but grow-ing concern and worked hard. However, against their better judgment the couple had purchased a home which they could not afford. They also entertained lavishly and beyond their means, with the result that they faced the possibility of losing everything they possessed.

We treated for the right solution to their dilemma. It seemed advisable that they should consult with a relative who had made a success of his business. At first pride held them back, but with continued treatment, they were willing to do whatever was necessary to solve the problem. The relative did not find fault with them, as they had expected, but he showed them the way out. He helped them sell the home, helped them work out a budget, and a plan to pay off their debts. After moving into modest quarters they both went to work to develop the business and it grew, and so did their income. As soon as they were willing to take right action, the demonstration followed.

"When wisdom entereth into thine heart, and
knowledge is pleasant unto thy soul:
"Discretion shall preserve thee, understanding
shall keep thee." Proverbs 2:10-11

CHAPTER 2

Have No False Gods

In the twentieth chapter of Exodus we find an interesting set of rules laid down centuries ago for the well-being of man. Because they teach man what not to do as well as what he should do, they are often considered ineffective and not too much attention is paid to them. They are known as THE TEN COMMANDMENTS.

They were not intended to be harsh directives and should not be regarded as such, but rather they should be looked upon as lights to guide man to the fulfillment of his desires for health, prosperity and well-being. They are mental aids to help man think better and direct his efforts to the attainment of his heart's desires, by seeking the guidance of Divine Mind at all times.

Surely it is as important at all times to know what not to do as well as to know what to do. Most cities are zoned, and if you plan to build a house, an office building, store or factory, you must first find out whether or not the zoning laws permit you to build the type of structure you have in mind, in the particular location in which you plan to erect it. Laws prohibit the adulteration of foods, excessive speed on highways; they prohibit the destruction of property, trespassing, etc. All such laws have been enacted for man's welfare.

A child is taught that it shall not cross the highway

when the traffic light is red, but wait until it turns green, which indicates that the crossing can be made with safety. The principles set down in Exodus are safeguards, to protect man from the error of his ways.

The writer of the commandments had no thought of taking the joy out of life, as some people are inclined to think. He simply said, "if you observe them you will stay out of trouble." Actually he ends on a cheerful, joyous note and holds out a wonderful promise. Here is what it says: "Ye shall walk in all the ways which the Lord your God hath commanded you, that ye may live, and that it may be well with you, and that ye may prolong your days in the land which the Lord your God hath commanded you, that ye may live, and that it may be well with you, and that ye may prolong your days in the land which ye shall possess." This promise is recorded in Deuteronomy 5:33. The commandments were considered so important by the writers of the Old Testament that we find them recorded not only in Exodus but also in Deuteronomy.

The first commandment states that we must be true to our spiritual nature, and unify with Divine Mind but not the false gods of our own creation. Let us remember that the word "false" means something that is misleading in appearance, is untrue and incorrect.

The graven images mentioned in the commandments are the materialistic tendencies within man that give power to things, instead of the Source from which they arise. Some graven images are tangible, such as houses, lands, jewels, money, furniture, investments, others are intangible, such as social position, status, career. There is always the danger of frittering away mental powers on things that have no intrinsic value. Material things are not evil in themselves, it is only when they take first place that they become false gods.

A man who had recovered from an illness that had hospitalized him for six weeks said, "I have a whole new sense of values now. I realize that many things are not nearly as important as I thought they were. One day I was sitting in the sun porch of the hospital and talked with the man who sat next to me. Our conversation drifted to automobiles. "Bill said, 'Joe, I have been doing a lot of thinking about myself. I took much better care of my automobile than I did myself. I had the oil and tires changed regularly, at the first sign of dust the car was washed; the mechanic checked it for any possible defects, but I paid very little attention to myself. In my desire to get ahead I drove myself so hard that I found myself in the hospital with a heart attack. I took better care of my car than I did myself, but that is going to change from here on.' "

The conversation made a great impression upon Joe and helped him change his own way of thinking. He continued by saying: "Like my friend in the hospital, I also took my health for granted and never thought I could get sick. I worked far into the night many times, forgot to eat, or just grabbed a sandwich and ate it in a hurry. The only thing that seemed important to me then was the money I was making, but I didn't consider the price I would have to pay.

"One of the first things I learned in the hospital was to eat regularly, which was something I had almost forgotten to do. I had time to think about other things than business. Why I even made new friends. I promised myself when I got well that I would find more time for my family, for recreation, and that I would start attending church regularly, and that is just what I am doing." Sickness is unpleasant but it can also be a valuable teacher.

When a certain ruler came to Jesus and asked him what to do to inherit eternal life, the first thing to which Jesus called his attention was the commandments. Jesus evidently held them in esteem. They must have been important to the ruler also, for he answered that he had kept them from his youth up. Then Jesus proceeded to tell him to distribute his wealth among the poor. Jesus never found fault with his wealthy friends or with wealth itself, it was only when he sensed that the possessions were overly important to the ruler, that he told him to part with them.

A woman with whom I discussed the commandments said to me: "Every child should be taught to memorize the commandments. I am always grateful that they were taught to me. I know and believe that God is Love but I also know that the right understanding of the commandments is good. I had a happy childhood, but I faced temptations as all young people do, and my knowledge of the commandments, and my willingness to live by them, kept me out of difficulties."

Jesus said the sabbath day was made for man and not man for the sabbath. A sabbath is a season or day of rest, and every one needs a period of rest, a change from the daily routine of living. It is a time to be made whole again, to be refreshed mentally and spiritually. Of course, one can pray anywhere, any place, and at any time, but there is something to be gained in putting forth the effort to attend a service in a House of Prayer that pays great dividends. It is an opportunity to cast the burdens on the Lord, to be free in mind, a time to be filled with inspiration, to forgive and to be forgiven.

One of the commandments that is probably broken more frequently than any other is the one pertaining to coveting. The commandment states very briefly but definitely that we do not have the slightest right to desire anything that belongs to another. That is making a false god of someone or something. Some people look forward to another's retirement to gain a desired position, others feel they have the right to take another person's time and make use of his talents and skills without adequate compensation; or they covet the houses, wealth, and lands of others.

10

Emerson said:

"And all that Nature made thy own,
Floating in air or pent in stone,
Will rive the hills and swim the sea
And, like thy shadow, follow thee."

Our own portion in life awaits us, and therefore there is no need to covet, claim or in any way desire what belongs to another. Right thinking and right action keep us from violating the great spiritual principles and thereby we gain our blessings.

Lao Tzu said:

"Do nothing by self-will, but rather conform to the Infinite Will, and everything will be done for you."

It is one thing to be tempted, another thing to yield to temptation. Ambition is wonderful as long as personal desires do not encroach upon others. Every person has the right to succeed, to be prosperous and have the finer things of life. They can be acquired in the right way, without desiring that which belongs to others.

Teachings similar to those laid down in Exodus and Deuteronomy were taught by the ancient Chinese. Let us ponder some of them.

"Take counsel how to put away your selfish thought."

"Teach your children not to deceive one another."

"If your conduct is injurious, it is cherished in your heart."

You do not need the wealth or property of others, you can demonstrate your own substance. You can create your own place in the world, if you are willing to put forth the necessary effort.

11

As we gain a greater understanding of the words: "I am the Lord thy God" we shall live so close to the One Presence, One Power, One Intelligence that nothing can move us. Once we know that the Christ self abides within us as our "hope and glory" the temptations and limitations of the outer world will be seen as shadows, and only the true light of love will motivate our thinking and actions.

CHAPTER 3

The Law of Increase

There is abundance for all of God's children, but each individual must bring forth his own supply. Great world teachers have proclaimed that the abundance that man desires the most is the good life. They have taught that all the keys to the good life, the bringing forth of abundance in the most desirable manner and form, are all within man's own being. Sometimes, when a person is experiencing difficulties, privations, or hardships of one kind or another, he may vehemently deny that this is true, but the fact remains that it is. Man often suffers because he has too many conflicting desires, too many personal wants, and until he decides what he wants most and goes to work to bring it forth, he is bound to suffer.

Every individual must come to grips with himself and put his attention on what he desires the most, work to attain it, and then the forces of his own being will move him toward achievement. He must make sure that he does not try to get what he wants at the expense of other people.

There is an innate goodness within every one that desires expression, a higher self that is interested in what is right, just, kind and true. If a person rides rough shod over others to attain his goal, or get what he wants, he is paving the way for difficulty for himself. He may cause trouble for others, but he will create the greatest difficulties for himself.

13

Inner goodness is a magnet. The more a person lives according to his spiritual nature the more he draws unto himself substance in the desired form, shape or manner that he needs for his own unfoldment and development. He exerts a fine influence then upon people and his environment. Only goodness can lift the world and the good person is a lifter, not a leaner. Goodness is also a fence, an invisible wall that protects the person who depends upon God.

Every individual should glory in the things that he can do well, and rejoice that he can be a blessing to others. I asked a friend who has been teaching school for many years if she finds teaching difficult. Her reply was, "I love children, and I love to teach them." She is very happy in her work, and instills high ideals in young minds. This woman is a tower of strength and when problems or difficulties arise, the children often turn to her for guidance. They have complete confidence in her. Her life is filled with joy and teaching is a wonderful, satisfying adventure for her.

When the power that we call "God" created this universe, abundance was provided for everyone. Because man has not aroused himself to take advantage of the supply that is his on every side there is still much distress and lack in the world. Man fears, and so withholds from himself and others what he should freely and abundantly share, namely, his love, friendship, kindness, goodness and his talents. Some people, having been hurt through misunderstandings or the unfairness of others, often come to the conclusion that all people are unkind and become aloof and withdrawn; they lose contact with people. They become so sensitive to a "great plenty" of disappointments that they miss the joy of living, and the "great plenty" of good that is all around them. It is a mistake to withdraw from the world because of disappointments. The power to change circumstances and conditions is within. It is not so much what happens to us as

14

the way we react to things that makes our lives happy or unhappy.

There are times of delays, disappointments, frustrations, and waiting that come to everyone, but that is part of life. The Buddha had a long, hard road to illumination but he received what he so earnestly sought. Jesus knew disappointments and heartache, but he overcame them, because he allowed the Christ within to govern his life.

Perhaps one of the most beautiful parables Jesus taught is that of the Good Samaritan. The Samaritan saw a fellow man in trouble and immediately gave the injured man aid, and paid for his food and lodging. Here was activity motivated by inner goodness, with no thought of reward or praise. What a glow of satisfaction the unknown benefactor must have had as he went on his way, rejoicing only in the thought of having done a kindness to someone who needed help.

Like attracts like. A consciousness of abundance attracts it. Money placed in a safe deposit box is out of circulation, like a buried talent, and draws no interest. Money wisely invested and kept in circulation draws more to it in the form of interest, increased dividends, or other increments.

Nature's wonderful way of perpetuating supply has given man endless opportunities to improve his way of life. Many methods have been devised to improve the soil and seeds, and in our country, we have learned to bring forth abundant crops. We are sharing this knowledge with other countries, so that want may disappear from the face of the earth. Food has its place and must be considered, but it alone should not be the object of man's existence.

Watching and observing birds in flight has taught man much and inspired him to invent airplanes that fly him from one place to another. Through oceanography he has learned to dive deeper and deeper into the great oceans and bring forth heretofore hidden knowledge about marine life, food in the oceans, and much more that will prove to be a boon to mankind. As man takes dominion of the land, sea, sky and air, he finds whole new worlds opening to him, new knowledge, beauty and abundance.

A person's first glimpse of the science of mind may result from a desire to learn more about the law of increase, and how to increase his prosperity. An unemployed person may seek spiritual help to find a new position, or additional income to take care of a family. Because of a pressing need and a great enthusiasm, these people often make quick demonstrations, but then they drop their studies, their daily treatments and wonder why they eventually face more problems. To prosper in the right way there must be a complete compliance with the law of right action, only in this way can lasting results be obtained. As the power of the mind is used in the right way, man's capacities and abilities increase accordingly, and he attracts the good that he really desires.

To comply with the Law of Increase, you must think increase, but allow it to come to you without interfering with the action of the Law. No permanent good can result from attempts to force a demonstration because the law cannot work contrary to its own nature. There is a great need in the world today to understand that prosperity results from right thinking and right action.

To prosper there must be a constant inflow and outflow, giving and receiving. Clear, fresh water comes from a stream that has both inlet and outlet. The law of increase may be likened unto a river. It may start off as a very small stream somewhere in the mountains, but it has a way of flowing over or around obstacles, continuing on its way, and increasing in size as it flows toward its outlet. Even the slightest increase in one's prosperity should be gratefully accepted. Gratitude has a way of increasing divine confidence, and this opens more doors to new opportunities and greater supply.

16

Opulence and affluence come in many forms. As we receive and satisfy our wants, we are in turn able to give as freely as we receive. Once wisdom is established in maintaining a balance between giving and receiving, we are capable of handling a greater inflow of supply; we can assume more responsibility, and this in turn results in greater prosperity.

Tithing or giving a tenth of one's substance to the Lord was known at the time of Abraham. He gave tithes to Melchizedek and became one of the richest men in the East. At Bethel Jacob vowed that he would give a tenth of all that was given to him, to the Lord. Jacob kept his promise, and despite the many tribulations he endured, he became a very wealthy man. Tithing is a way of keeping supply in circulation. It develops a feeling of security in the individual, an inner satisfaction, that supply is constant and ever available. The tithes that man gives, whether in time, money or possessions, do not always return to him from the sources to which he gives them, but they return with increase through the outworking of the Divine Law, which gives to each his own. By complying with the law, and trusting it, he becomes affluent, and riches come to him, regardless of circumstances or appearances.

People sometimes ask why they should tithe, why give a tenth to the Lord's work. A tenth given to the Lord's work is the best way to support a church or spiritual institution. Tithing helps keep the church's and the individual's finances in a healthy condition. It has always worked in the lives of people who put it into practice. There are many people today who have proved that tithing is the answer to true prosperity. Some people try it for a while and then stop, if they do not get immediate results. It is by applying the rule consistently over a long period of time that it proves its true worth. To give a tenth just to get is using the law for selfish purposes. It should be given in a spirit of gratitude

17

for blessings received and to be received. When the tithe is given in a generous and loving manner, it begins to increase at once.

Prosperity does not necessarily depend upon money. It should be based upon ideals, fresh ideas and service. Money represents earnings, wages, and purchasing power. It can purchase commodities, luxuries, homes, automobiles, machinery, and many other things. Because it is a powerful medium of exchange it should be managed carefully. Tithing helps one gain that knowledge.

"Large streams from little fountains flow,
Tall oaks from little acorns grow."
David Everett

There is no substitute for industry, honesty and the intelligent use of one's talents. The law of increase demands that we give our attention to new ideas and live in the present, not the past. Most people enjoy window shopping. An attractive store window attracts potential customers. Someone looking in a store window, seeing the merchandise attractively displayed, may have no thought of making any purchases at that particular time, but something he sees may stir him to own it and his mind begins to move toward the object. Even though he may not purchase it at the time, if he likes it, he has dropped the desire into his subconscious, and may find himself returning to the store to purchase the item.

The following steps are helpful in maintaining a prosperity consciousness:

1. Turn to Divine Mind for guidance before embarking upon any new enterprise.
2. Do not think lack or defeat. Establish a sound consciousness of success and expect it.
3. Render some worthwhile service.

4. Do not overextend when opening a business. Enlarge when it can be done without strain or struggle.
5. Be patient and build good will.
6. Appreciate and value new ideas. Be on the alert for them.
7. Express appreciation for little favors and little things as well as big ones.

The man or woman who presents a new idea to the world does not always meet with immediate success. It may require time for a new idea to take hold, for people to glimpse the possibilities that are enfolded within it. It is told of Zoroaster, the founder of the great Persian religion, which flourished years ago, that he had to wait ten years for his first convert, then the idea began to take hold and the new religion became a mighty force.

Thought should be given to increase the capacity to enjoy life. Merely to work to increase wealth or money or possessions can become a drudgery, but to increase the capacity to enjoy life can turn into a great adventure. As the spirit of joy enters into the thinking and feeling nature, the real meaning of the word "prosperity," which denotes a state of well being, becomes alive.

To live constantly with worry often brings illness in its wake, and conditions instead of improving, grow worse. The solution to the problem is a true understanding of prosperity, its nature, what it really is. The law of prosperity is consistent and demands that income and outgo be considered together. It is better to have a reputation for paying one's bills than to attempt to create an illusion of wealth and worry about debts. Isaiah was not only a great prophet but also a very practical person and his teachings, if followed, can be profitable. The advice he gave the people of his day holds good for us also. He said, "Wherefore do ye spend money for that which is not bread? and your labor for that

19

which satisfieth not? hearken diligently unto me, and eat ye that which is good." Isaiah 55:2.

True wealth is a quality of mind, a firm belief that substance is ever-existing and ever-available. There is a substance that is spiritual, infinite, inexhaustible out of which all forms are made. The more skillfully we learn to handle our thinking, the more supply and beauty we can bring into expression. If we do not always succeed the first time, we can always try again.

Prosperity does not necessarily mean the same thing to all people. A book collector may feel very gratified if he finds himself in possession of a rare volume, or a collection he has desired for a long time; while a musician may feel elated if he can purchase a fine instrument. A lover of paintings or sculptures, on the other hand, may rejoice to own a masterpiece or a work of art that he greatly admires. A strong desire for something that seems unattainable at the moment, is often gratified in the most unexpected manner, providing there is faith in the law of increase.

A woman saw a necklace and earrings in the window of a jewelry store and liked them very much. She wanted to purchase the jewelry but found that her funds were insufficient, so she dismissed the thought, but every now and then it popped up and she found herself wishing for a new necklace and earrings. One morning, while quietly giving thanks for all the blessings she had received, she suddenly had the feeling that she would receive a present. About an hour later a friend brought her a gift. When she opened the box, to her great joy, her wish was granted. The box contained a beautiful necklace and matching earrings. Although the friend did not know that she wanted jewelry, Divine Mind brought fulfillment.

Another student of the science of mind had a nice purse which she had purchased and used for a very short time. A friend who saw the purse admired it very much and she gave it to her. The friend was elated and the student thought nothing more of the incident, being happy that it had brought joy to someone. She thought about purchasing another purse the next time she went to town. Her trip to town was delayed and in the meantime she was given three new purses. Then she said, "Thank you, Father, I have enough." Her good flowed lavishly and abundantly because she had shared. She was not interested in hoarding and gave thanks when her needs were more than met.

A young widow found that her funds were almost exhausted after she paid her husband's medical and funeral bills. She wondered how she could support herself and her young son, but faith came to her rescue. Knowing the allness of God she prayed for guidance. She made a list of everything she could do in the way of earning a livelihood for herself and son. It was revealed to her that the small town in which she lived needed a business college. She had taught school prior to her marriage and reached the decision to use her teaching skills to bring in an income. The school was started in an old building, and all the equipment was secondhand, but with a brave heart she started her new venture.

Being a capable and conscientious person, she taught well and the students recommended her enthusiastically. Step by step her school grew. As more students enrolled she replaced the old equipment with new, added teachers to her faculty, and offered more courses of study. Eventually the school was moved into a new building.

In the beginning it was necessary for her to cook, wash, iron, teach, prepare lessons and grade papers, as well as look after her growing son, but she never complained and was grateful for every sign of growth. Her strength was renewed by daily spiritual treatment. She made a valuable contribution to the community and her income grew and grew.

This teacher worked diligently and used her income with

discretion. As the school grew and the larger quarters were required she received the inner guidance that the time had arrived to "Enlarge the place of thy tent, and let them stretch forth the curtains of thine habitations: spare not, lengthen thy cords, and strengthen thy stakes." Isaiah 52:2. This she was able to do easily and without worry. Remember: "If you work with God you will always get a bonus."

When the outer looks dark and dismal and lack seems apparent, it is well to return to the indwelling source of all substance and fill the mind and soul with spiritual food. All through the Bible runs the promise, that God will provide, will increase, not only money, food, shelter, and clothing, but he will provide employment, heal disease and increase the health of his people. "The Lord thy God shall bless thee in all thine increase, and in all the works of thine hands, therefore thou shalt surely rejoice." Deuteronomy 16:15.

I render unto Caesar the things that are Caesar's and unto God the things that are God's. I have a "great plenty". Every need is supplied, God blesses me with wisdom and knowledge; riches and wealth increase. I praise and give thanks.

CHAPTER 4

The Divine Urge

There is a divine urge in everything in creation, something which says, "Come up higher, there are new horizons, new unconquered worlds." The urge to know more about the universe has encouraged man to sail the oceans and lakes in search of new waterways, to travel across wilderness and desert, and climb the highest mountains. To help him accomplish his purposes he has built more seaworthy ships, submarines and pleasure boats; automobiles, trucks and pleasure cars of all types, and railroads. Not content with that, he has built airplanes and jets, has set foot on the moon, and thinks in terms of inter-planetary travel.

Man has an innate curiosity to know as much as possible about the world in which he lives. He stretches his mind and reaches far beyond the immediate sphere of his existence into the vast reaches of space. The One Mind that controls the starry spaces is the same mind that brought man into being, and moves through him; and he is always making a greater effort to unify with this One Mind.

The desire to remain youthful, healthy, alert and finally overcome death, has motivated man to learn more about himself and his universe. He has sought ways and means in the outer. Ponce de Leon searched for the legendary Fountain of Youth. Other explorers of mind have used meditation; while still others have looked to herbs, fruits and exer-

23

cise as a way of attainment. What man needs to remember is that he is a spiritual being, made in the image and likeness of God. The power is in the inner, not the outer. However, since he lives in two worlds, the eternal and the transitory, he has his share of conflicts to resolve.

The outer world presses upon him its gifts of money, wealth, position, fame, and prestige, while the inner urges him to accept his priceless spiritual heritage. Until he learns to accept the inner as the real, and allows it to move him forward, he will encounter frustrations and disappointments. He has learned that he can improve his lot in the world of phenomena and is faced with the fact that it is constantly changing, while the spiritual is changeless. He has improved crops, plants, machines, drained swamps, irrigated arid land, created artificial lakes. These are steps he is taking to improve his environment, lengthen his life-span and increase his wealth.

We would not want the same lamps, coal stoves or horse drawn carriages of bygone years. Actually we greet improvements and changes and expect them. Old homes and buildings are torn down and newer and better buildings erected. This satisfies the urge to beautify, improve and bring forth something better.

Not only does man have the urge to improve his life and environment but he also has a desire to let future generations share in his gains. Great sculptures have been a way in which he has been able to depict his progress and fulfill his need for self-expression. Monuments, obelisks, pyramids and sculptures of various kinds have withstood the ravages of the elements for centuries. They have enabled us to understand how people of past generations lived and thought. At first they worshipped many gods and goddesses, but gradually came to the worship of one God. Slowly but surely man has been developing his great potential.

The divine urge expresses as instinct in birds. A pair of

robins had built a nest each year on the ledge of the front porch of a home owned by a bird loving family. The narrow ledge was located between one of the porch pillars and the roof. The house was eventually sold and the new family knew nothing about the robins and their nest. One morning they found the porch littered with bits of straw, grass and string. They swept it away and the next morning the same sight greeted them. They could not understand this and then detected the robins building their nest. The string and grass had been blown down by a gust of wind. Fearing that predatory animals might kill their young, the family tried to discourage the robins from building their nest on the ledge.

The following morning the birds had moved their nest to the other side of the porch. Impressed with the determination of their little feathered friends, the family relented. After the young birds were in the nest a cat attempted to reach them but the birds made such a racket the cat left the scene. In their efforts to fly the young birds first wobbled about on the porch but each day they gained strength and finally flew away. The robins stayed close to the house because they felt safe. Their songs expressed their appreciation. "And the birds of the air have nests." Matthew 8:20.

Nature, too, is constantly allowing the divine urge to move her forward, and the face of the earth is always changing. One evening, while staying at a hotel that was located at the edge of a forest, I observed a storm coming up. Lightning streaked across the sky and lighted up the entire area. The trees groaned and moaned as the storm rumbled along and at times terrific crashes rent the air as though the earth were being swallowed up. The wind pelted the rain against the windows and I wondered if the glass could withstand the onslaught. Finally the storm subsided and the morning broke clear and bright.

I walked into the forest in the early morning hours to see the effects of the storm. The air was fragrant with the scent of wood. The leaves on the trees had a clean, fresh look, but many dead twigs and branches were lying on the ground. It was Nature's way of clearing out that which had served its purpose. She had breathed new life and growth into the forest and filled the streams and healed the parched earth. The birds were singing and the squirrels and chipmunks scampering everywhere. ". . . the Lord has his way in the whirlwind and storm." Nahum 1:3.

A fine young man with the urge to help people and suc-ceed in his own profession, accomplished his purpose in an unusual way. He was a member of a large family and had to earn money to continue his education. He worked after school hours, during vacations and while attending law col-lege. He never lost sight of his goal. After graduating from college he enlisted in the navy and served his country.

Returning to civilian life he did not have enough money to maintain a law office. Undaunted he looked around for a job and became a salesman in a department store. He was so pleasant and courteous that he made fine headway as a salesman and opened an office in his home where he coun-seled clients in the evenings. Finally he was able to devote his full time to the practice of law and prospered. "Train up a child in the way he should go: and when he is old, he will not depart from it."

Sometime during the eleventh century B.C. a shepherd boy sat on a hillside watching his sheep. Something within urged him to express the glory of creation all around him. Day after day he watched the sun rise and set. He wondered about the vastness of the starry firmament; and so on the Judean hillside the Psalms began to take shape within his mind.

He was a good shepherd. His sheep followed him gladly and obeyed his voice, for he guarded and tended them well. He kept them safe from wild animals and saw to it that they had food and fresh water. He kept them from falling into

26

deep crevices or ravines. When they were injured or bruised he tenderly cared for them until they recovered. Day and night he watched over them to see that no evil would befall them. And he thought about all these things when he looked into the star-filled sky.

The nature of God absorbed a great part of his thought and he expressed his faith in words and music. The twenty-third Psalm is the one in which he likens God unto a great Shepherd, tenderly and lovingly watching over his people. God for him was not far away, but close at hand, and David felt sure God loved his creation with an infinite love.

After David another great man came along to influence the hearts and minds of men and women. He did not try to force his viewpoints upon people, but by means of parables and stories he taught them to change their thinking. Jesus had a great ideal and his deep desire was to help people express their own divinity. He wanted them to enjoy health, peace and prosperity and he told them to seek these things in the kingdom within them. He healed, taught and blessed people, and spoke in simple, understandable language.

Despite chaotic conditions in the world, more and more people are learning to apply the teachings of Jesus through the science of mind, and their correct thinking is bearing fruit.

When God created man in His own image and likeness and breathed into him the breath of life he became a living soul and the divine urge took over. Man felt a stirring within to express himself; to fulfill his divine destiny, to show forth his divinity, his greatness. Sometimes he seems to forget, but the urge is always there, influencing him to be true to the best within him. It sent Albert Schweitzer into hot, torrid Africa, to bring healing and a better way of life to people. It sent Admiral Byrd to the South Pole to set up a weather station to make flying safer. Wherever we find people working for the betterment of the race, the divine urge is leading them on. Regardless of hardships or discomforts they have a goal to achieve and work ever toward its fulfillment. When heeded, the divine urge points the way to man's life work so that he can use his talents and skills for the glory of God and his own joy.

The divine urge helps man in his struggle to free himself from his self-inflicted bonds of poverty, despair, illness, pain and suffering. It helps him survive in the face of seemingly impossible obstacles. Spurred on by the divine urge men have survived ship wreck, hunger, thirst, heat, cold, poverty, earthquakes, floods, and disasters of all kind. Something within him says: "You are greater than you think. You can overcome. Trust in God, have faith in the divine within you, and you will conquer." It is this inner prompting that helps man hold on until the victory is won.

Divine Mind is ever urging me to express the best and finest within me. It keeps me from error and leads me into paths of righteousness. I follow the leadings of Truth and my success is assured.

CHAPTER 5

Word Power

Have you ever pondered the tremendous power of words? If so, have you stopped to think what a blessing your vocabulary is; what wonders words perform for you? Through your ability to use words aright you communicate your thoughts to others, make known your wants, aspirations, dreams, the things that you hope to achieve. Through this avenue of communication you receive countless blessings.

Some primitive tribes have vocabularies consisting of as few as eighty words, whereas the vocabulary of an educated man or woman consissts of thousands of words. Since words are so powerful it is important to say the right thing at the right time. This practice is commended in the Bible. Proverbs says: "A word fitly spoken is like apples of gold in pictures of silver."

As man moves more and more into an age of automation, air travel, and potential space travel, he finds himself face to face with the need of increasing his vocabulary to keep abreast of the happenings of his times. New words are constantly being coined as man moves into new dimensions of thinking and progress.

We can learn much about a person if we will pay attention to the words he uses. All professions and vocations have words that are unique and students and apprentices must learn well the words which apply to the field in which they wish to earn a livelihood. Everyone devotes more time than he realizes to the learning of new words.

A musician's vocabulary contains many words applicable to the composition, writing and interpreting of music. Knowing the various meanings of words peculiar to his profession enables him to express the endless degrees of shading and feeling so essential to the interpretation of any fine musical composition. A discriminating musician knows that the directions printed on the sheet of music are really a part of the soul of the composition. By following them a pianist, violinist, vocalist, or instrumentalist knows what the composer intended to convey to others, through the medium of music. The mastery of musical terms aids the musician in acquiring the feel of the composition so that the interpretation he presents to his audience stirs the heart and soul. The eloquence of music can bring healing to a troubled heart and mind.

A competent artist must be acquainted with the names of a great variety of paints, the names of the best brushes, the finest of oils and water colors, so that he may purchase and use those that are lasting. As he contemplates a new work of art he must determine whether it will be done in oil or water color, whether it will be a seascape, a still life, portrait, or a miniature. He thinks in terms of colors, blues, greens, reds, browns, and many interrelated shades. He must think in terms of form, perspective, and dimension, so again the power of words comes into play. When the artist places his works on the market, either he or a competent sales person must be able to discuss the merits of the respective works of art in an intelligent manner with prospective buyers.

Symbols are sometimes used in place of words. When an engineer is about to build a bridge he makes a number of drawings showing lines and numerous markings. To one versed in the interpretation of the drawings they tell a story.

30

They tell a story of size, weight, strength, length, and the many other things needed to build a strong, substantial bridge.

A person interested in the culinary art collects cook books because they contain the recipes of many peoples of many climes, and make it possible for the skilled cook to present a variety of meals that would not otherwise be possible were it not for the written word. Knowing the names of vegetables, herbs, flours, and other ingredients facilitates the process of reducing the written word into something tangible like a new pudding, cake, or casserole dinner. Thus, familiarity with words makes it possible for a person to work more efficiently and with less stress and strain.

Man's desire to improve his status, to promote his welfare, and have a better life, has caused him to bring into expression root words, and from them he has formed many others to fit his expanding mental and spiritual world. His desire to express his thoughts and his feelings to others has resulted in the art of writing and drawing, the printing press, the typewriter, and many other inventions to expedite this process. Man can now communicate very readily with his fellowman at distant points by means of letters, telephone, telegrams, radio, or cablegram.

The power of speech is one of the greatest gifts God has bestowed upon man. But let us remember that this power can be abused as well as used. Since words have power, you can use them for your betterment or for your detriment. The right use of words is spoken of as a blessing in the Bible, and the wrong use, as a curse. The twenty-eighth chapter of Deuteronomy is interesting reading. The first fourteen verses are filled with blessings and promises of God's goodness to those who work with the spiritual law and use the power of the word intelligently and spiritually. The following verses which speak of the curse remind man that he must not abuse his divine heritage. It is a warning that if man uses

31

his great gifts selfishly and turns the power of the word against himself he is violating God's laws and will gather thistles instead of roses.

Words can stimulate progress, health, and prosperity if used as a blessing. Where the power of the word has been used to bless it has brought great advance in civilization. In the New Testament Jesus vividly calls to mind the need for using the right words. He, more than anyone, knew the potency of words and said: "By your words ye are justified and by your words ye are condemned." If you have spoken in haste or someone has said something unkind to you, do not harbor the unpleasant words. Forgive them, wipe the slate of your mind clean. It can be done through the word "forgiveness." Forgive yourself and forgive the other person, then forget it. Remember, if words have power to wound they also have great power to harmonize and to heal.

The glorious prophet Isaiah made this striking statement: "The Lord hath given me the tongue of the learned, that I should know how to speak a word in season to him that is weary." A word of encouragement, who can measure it? It may mean the difference between success and defeat, it may be the turning point for a friend, a loved-one, or someone whom God has sent your way. Very often it is the biggest gift, the greatest blessing you can bestow.

Jesus Christ did not try to impress people with his erudition. The Master Teacher used simple words that were easily understood and yet they contained the greatest truths ever presented to the world. Those power-filled words, spoken long ago are with us still, reminding us that we must discipline the mind and the tongue. Let us consider one of the beatitudes: "Blessed are the meek (the teachable) for they shall inherit the earth." Think on these words. If you are teachable, if you are willing to learn new truths each day, yours is a rich inheritance. You shall inherit the earth. What a rich inheritance is yours! It is filled with treasures, it supplies you with food, a place to live, a place on which to plant your feet, a place to work and grow and learn. All the raw materials are there for your use.

Let us go back for a minute to the Old Testament and see what it says about the inheritance that Jesus mentions. If you want to learn more about it begin with the twenty-eighth chapter of Job and read through chapter thirty-nine, and this beatitude will take on a new meaning for you. Here is set forth some real food for thought. There is mention of the vein of silver, a place for gold, sapphires, onyx, coral, rubies, pearl, crystal, topaz, the abundance of waters, clouds, light, snow, cold, frost, morning stars, Pleiades, Arcturus; the beasts of the field, the fowl of the air. Too often these magnificent creations are taken for granted, yet how rich we are just to know about them.

In the reading matter we also find some wonderful promises: "If they obey and serve him, they shall spend their days in prosperity, and their years in pleasure." If you obey and serve God you shall spend your days in a state of continual well-being, which is true prosperity. To lay hold of true prosperity you cannot fill your mind with thoughts of lack, nor speak lack. You must change your words and your thinking. Remember you are important to God. He created you in his own image and after his own likeness. "Behold, God is mighty, and despiseth not any; he is mighty in strength and power."

Now let us return again to Jesus and the power of the word. A centurion came to Jesus and asked him to heal his servant. The centurion was a man of great faith and understanding and said to Jesus: ". . . but speak the word only, and my servant shall be healed." Jesus spoke the word and the servant was healed. He did not require the presence of the servant to bring about a healing. He spoke the healing word and health was established. He blessed the loaves and fishes and the multitude was fed. Jesus spoke words filled with spirit and life and immediately a corresponding action took place. Everyone has the power within to use words effectively, to speak words of encouragement, healing, prosperity and goodwill. To get the desired results the words should be spoken from a pure and holy heart and mind, from the Christ center where they are energized with goodwill and love.

What kind of vocabulary are you building? One of praise and gratitude, one of encouragement, healing, love and peace? If not, begin now to bless your world. Every word is important.

As you grow daily in your appreciation of the power of words and have a greater awareness of the magnificent possibilities they contain, new spiritual horizons will appear. Heed the admonitions of Isaiah and of Jesus and speak only words of joy, health, love, good-will, forgiveness, harmony and prosperity. They will bring you an abundance of good, a rich harvest of spiritual values. Not only will you raise your own consciousness but that of the entire world. Each person contributes his share to the good or ill of the world. Use your words to bless.

(Published Spring issue 1959 New Thought Quarterly)

CHAPTER 6

Orderly Thinking

The Science of Mind teaches that man has a conscious or objective mind and a subjective mind, sometimes called the subconscious. It also teaches that there is only ONE MIND, but that these terms or definitions are used to describe the activities of the mind.

Sometimes terms are confusing and a little help from the dictionary makes it easier to understand what the conscious and subconscious planes of mind are and how they function. The dictionary says that the word "subjective" means having the nature of or pertaining to a subject. Now let us see what "subject" means. The definition is "to cause to lie beneath; to bring under control of or dominion, to throw under." Ernest Holmes' definition is: "The inner side, Subconscious."

The word "conscious" as described in *A Dictionary of Pastoral Psychology* edited by Virgilius Ferm give this definition: "When one is aware of his mental content, he is said to be conscious. That portion, therefore, of the mind's content of which we are aware is said to be the 'conscious.' "

Now then, when the conscious mind is doing the job that it should be doing, we are conscious of our surroundings; we know what we are thinking, we know what we are doing. The subconscious picks up what we are thinking and deposits it within the storehouse of the mind. Since it is under the dominion and authority of the conscious mind, it must do what it is told. It does not of itself decide, "this is not good for me; this will not help me," it has no such choice. That is definitely the work of the conscious mind.

If we are not careful of what we store up, then we must not complain if we do not like the results that come to us from time to time. If we are not careful we can gather a lot of dust and "sweep it under the rug" mentally. It may be out of sight but it is still there. Some day the room must be cleaned and the dust swept from under the rug. In the same manner that a room must be cleaned there comes a time when the mental dust and disorderly thinking must be cleaned out. It requires daily mental house cleaning to think lucidly.

Do you say, "I have a poor memory, I can't remember?" Why not? You can do something about it. Tell yourself that you have a perfect memory. If you find you are not ready to cope with the word "perfect" use the word "good," perhaps you like that a little better to begin with. Then tell yourself that you will pay attention to the things you should remember. Memory requires attention. Start by strengthening your powers of observation. When you walk to the store to pick up groceries and ice cream take a good look at the houses on the street, notice the trim, the type of windows, the house numbers, the lawns, and when you come home recall what you have observed. Before long you will find yourself remembering instead of forgetting. Make it a strong point to remember the pleasant things, not the unpleasant ones. Look at what you are seeing.

I know a woman who had a very limited education. She went to elementary school for three years and yet she has a very interesting life. For years her income was very meager and she did all kinds of work to support herself; and then, at an age when most people think of retiring she learned how to operate a typewriter, not rapidly, but sufficiently well to address envelopes; she also learned simple office procedures. With the help of a few interested friends she learned how to groom herself so that she looks smart and chic. Slowly she educated herself and her income has steadily increased. To-day she lives in a nice apartment and has a host of friends. At one time she could not even spell, but life has taken on a new meaning and even her posture has improved. Such is the power of the mind and such are the capabilities of a person who has the will and the determination to improve.

Thinking can be considered mental and spiritual food. What we feed the mind we tend to bring forth in our life and affairs. If we feed on truth, think truth, beauty, health, kindness, love, wealth, and kindred ideas, then we have some-thing substantial to depend upon. On the other hand, if we foster envy, anger, jealousy, fear, insecurity, lack of faith, deception, or anything that is contrary to our highest good, it crops out. "For as he thinketh in his heart, so is he." Proverbs 23:7. It is not only how you think about some-thing, but how you feel about it that counts.

Now someone may ask, "Why is it so important that I think right every moment of the day and night, what differ-ence does it make?" As a child you were sent to school for the purpose of learning to think and to acquire knowledge. If you paid attention to what you were taught you did not have too much trouble with examinations, but if you spent time day-dreaming you found examinations difficult.

The subconscious mind is a real blessing, necessary to life, to thinking, but it should be treated as a close relative, and not as an unwanted alien. When we love the members of our family we want the very best for them. Why not give our subconscious mind the very best kind of thinking? It is so loyal, so faithful, such a good servant; it deserves good treatment, respect, and recognition.

Another person asks, "What about all the evil in the world?" We have to agree there is much that needs to be done to make this world a better place in which to live, but the elimination of evil begins with the individual. To the extent that you, as an individual, eliminate evil from your thinking, to that extent you are helping to bring about a better world. After all, the world is composed of one and one and one. All individuals think their own thoughts, and the concern should not be with what the other person is thinking, but with what you as an individual are thinking. "But the wisdom that is from above is first pure, then peaceable, gentle, and easy to be intreated, full of mercy and good fruits, without partiality, and without hypocrisy. And the fruits of righteousness is sown in peace of them that make peace." James 3:17-18.

If we read a little further in the book of James we are told in the fourth chapter to "purify our hearts," which means our emotions. This seems like a big order and so it is, but then anything as important as clear thinking, deserves our utmost attention. Think how much precious time, energy, and thinking is wasted in gossip, ugly rumors, discussions of illness, lack, poverty, that should be diverted into constructive channels.

How do you go about setting your mental house in order? Start with a little habit. Suppose you have difficulty in getting up in the morning and are inclined to be grumpy. Sit down and talk it over with yourself. Why do you dislike to get up in the morning? Do you stay up too late at night? Do you dislike your work? If you stay up too late, resolve definitely and positively that you will remedy the condition. Be firm with yourself. Deny yourself an expensive luxury that causes you difficulty. If you read too long, look at the clock and resolutely put the book away. Perhaps you need to turn off the radio or television. Do not give yourself the excuse, "I just want to see how this ends," or "just five minutes more won't hurt." Discipline yourself, teach yourself to go to bed on time. Set your clock and when the alarm goes off, get up. You may not feel like it at first, but make the effort, after a while it will become a subconscious habit, and your wonderful mind will prove to be your ideal servant.

Start your day with a good treatment. Read one of the beautiful Psalms. Fill your mind to the brim with good thoughts. Be kind, overlook all the minor irritations that arise; treat people with courtesy and kindness. Do not grab the spotlight. Be fair. People are necessary to your success. Make it a mental habit to think joy, health, prosperity, peace, progress, and see what a difference it makes. Thank God for being ALIVE. Declare fervently and reverently: "I will praise thee; for I am fearfully and wonderfully made; marvellous are thy works; and that my soul knoweth right well." Psalm 139:14.

(Published in winter edition 1968 *New Thought Quarterly*.)

CHAPTER 7

Hidden Treasures

The science of mind, which is the science of clear think-ing, is helping man to discover the riches of mind. To un-cover this wealth it is necessary to quiet the mind and enter the inner sanctuary, the secret place of the Most High. No resentment, worry or anxious thoughts should be carried into this inner shrine. When you are relaxed use a treatment or read some beautiful Psalms or an inspiring book. Your spiritual treatment can be one of peace, illumination or con-fidence. If you have the patience to make this a daily habit you can then learn what Spirit reveals to you. You will not always receive inspiration, but you will receive strength and courage to perform your daily work. When you do receive spiritual inspiration it will always lead you into the right direction.

One evening I asked the students in one of my classes if anyone had an experience he or she would like to share that would be of help to others. A man who was a newcomer spoke up and said that he had learned a big lesson in church the previous Sunday. He went on to say that I had brought out the fact that resentment always hurts the person who harbors it, and health and supply can be impaired if it is not removed.

The student said a ray of light entered his mind at the time. For many years he had resented several people who had been unfair and unkind to him. He suddenly decided that if his health was to be restored, and he was to succeed in a new business he had just started, he would have to remove the ill-will and replace it with good will. That is what he did and he became very successful, when he got rid of his mental burdens. When he put his attention on the constructive side of life he began to think clearly. As long as his mind was in turmoil he could not reach a satisfactory conclusion. When the turmoil subsided and inspiration took over he saw everything in a different light.

A woman moved into a home that was surrounded on all sides by a yard that had been neglected. There were lovely shade trees, shrubs and plants, but they needed to be trimmed, and endless weeds had overrun the place, so she immediately set to work to put the yard in order. Each day she cleared away some weeds, cut back dead branches, loosened the soil, and in time the results were gratifying.

Her biggest difficulty was removing a vine that had taken over an entire corner of the walk leading to one of the entrances to the house. When she removed the vine she uncovered a shrub that was quite large, but had almost been smothered. A portion had withered, but with care it began to revive. However, in a few weeks the vine made another attempt to take over. This time she disentangled the roots of the vine from the shrub, and at last it was free to receive sufficient nourishment from the earth and air. She brought the beauty of her thinking into the outer, and considered the shrub one of her garden treasures.

Inharmonious thoughts, like the creeping vine, are devastating. If allowed to spread unhindered they can do untold damage. The roots of discontent must be cleared out and care taken that they do not re-enter the mind.

Some people are too lazy and indifferent to bring forth their inner riches. A young woman secured a position in an office shortly after graduating from high school. At first she thought about continuing her education at an evening school and then gave up the idea because she thought it was too much trouble to learn at night. She held the same position year after year and wondered why she was never promoted. She did nothing to improve herself and became very unhappy and discontented.

One day calamity struck. The firm for which she had worked for years closed its doors and she was without employment. After many weary weeks of searching for employment she finally sought spiritual help. I asked her if she had tried prayer and she said that she had not prayed nor entered a church for a long time, but she was willing to put forth the effort to pray and would return to church and she carried through. She was told to return in a week and report progress. During the week she had the urge to return to one of the employment agencies and asked the counselor why she was having so much difficulty in securing a position. The counselor advised her to return to school for a refresher course and learn new office techniques. A few months later she was ready to leave business school and found a new position waiting for her. She earned more salary than she had at any time before. Her mental outlook improved and her progress continued.

The prophet Haggai said, "consider your way." The subconscious mind needs recognition and respect if it is to work efficiently. It can also do what it is directed to do. Had the young woman disregarded the urge to return to the counselor she would not have solved her problem, but when she "considered her way" turned about face, she took the right action. Her larger income did not start immediately, but when she prepared herself to receive it the way opened for her success.

Franz Schubert gave the world great musical treasures. He wrote some of the most beautiful songs ever written. Poetry provided much of his inspiration. It has been said of him that he did more than any other composer to weld music and poetry. He brought them together in a glorious unity of form.

Schubert realized that he would have to expend effort to perpetuate the beautiful melodies that came to him from the hidden depths of his own being, and he made it a habit to devote his mornings to composing. Fifteen years, morning after morning, he worked, writing down the musical thoughts that came winging their way to him. He was such a skillful composer that his compositions required no revision, although most composers of his day made preliminary sketches of their compositions and then revised them. He was truly a genius and his mind handed him the compositions in their finished form.

Schubert enriched the musical thought of the world by the beautiful melodies he gave to it, but he never learned the great Biblical truth that "the laborer deserves his wages." Schubert was very poor and ill many times for lack of food. He had very little business ability and lacked tact. He did not get along well with people. Had he used the wonderful powers of his mind to help him, not only in composing music, but in every phase of his life, he could have been adequately compensated.

Tact is essential in getting along with people. The tactful person is the one who establishes good will, who is sensitive to the other person's problems, as well as his own. Tact is not insincere flattery. It consists in right thinking about others, saying things that are kind and truthful. Tact overcomes barriers, dissolves antagonisms and creates harmony. The mind of the tactful person is centered in Truth, dwells on beauty and brings it into visibility.

There is no need to suffer privations to bring forth an ideal. There is enough in the Universal Storehouse for everyone. Learn to avail yourself of it through spiritual treatment and prayer. At one time it was thought that a genius had to be poor; that poverty improved his work, but that is

44

a fallacy. There may have been times when hunger spurred an individual to work and produce, when he would not have done so otherwise. Remember that the mind that is capable of bringing forth rich ideas, can depend upon Divine Mind for adequate compensation as well.

Harry Granison Hill wrote in his book "Rational Religion":

> "We know that we are truly and fundamentally religious because something within us responds and thrills as the finger of God touches lightly upon the strings of our hearts, and a low, sweet prelude rises like faint music and subtly lifts us into rhythms of responsive emotion, and we can almost visualize our atonement with the Invisible, while our whole being throbs in tune with the Infinite."

Children share their joys spontaneously. A young boy with a deep love for nature, surpassed only by his love for his family, awoke one spring morning and saw some wild flowers blooming in a lot to the rear of his home. Quietly he slipped out of the house and barefooted he walked across the muddy ground until he reached the flowers. Carefully he picked a bouquet. Just as the family was beginning to wonder why he was late for breakfast his young sister looked out of the dining room window and saw her brother plucking the flowers. A few minutes later a mud-covered boy walked into the kitchen with shining eyes and presented the flowers to his mother. Graciously she accepted them, thanked him and kissed his mud-covered face. The flowers were placed in a vase for all to enjoy. No one mentioned the muddy tracks on the kitchen floor, the mud wiped into the towels, nor his mud-covered clothing. The family saw only a loving young heart and a loving deed.

Destructive habits in children can often be cured if they are given something they can cherish. A woman harassed by young children who pulled up the flowers in her garden and threw stones whenever they had an opportunity decided to solve the problem with kindness, but each time she approached the children they ran.

One morning when a tousle-headed youngster started tearing up the flowers, she held a package in her hands and called to him saying, "Would you like a present?" He ran toward her as fast as he could, and suddenly five more children were reaching out their hands for a gift. To each child she gave a small framed picture with a Biblical scene. Before the end of the day twenty children arrived at her home, asking for pictures. She had to purchase more in order to meet the demand, but a wonderful friendship was established. No longer were plants destroyed, nor stones thrown in gardens.

Where a love for beauty is fostered in a home the children appreciate and care for their possessions. I received a dinner invitation from a family that was moving to another city. After the table blessing had been given by the oldest son, the young daughter looked up at me with a big smile and said, "Mother used her best table cloth, napkins and dishes today because you were coming. We don't use them every day. We save them for company." I told the little one I appreciated their thoughtfulness and felt very honored. The little girl said "thank you" and the rest of the family smiled. That was the child's way of telling me the family had shared their treasures with me and we had a wonderful evening together. "For where your treasure is, there will your heart be also." Matt. 6:21.

> I rejoice that I can forever draw upon the inexhaustible storehouse of God for treasures of heart, mind and soul. I rejoice each day for I am blessed with new, rich, wonderful ideas. Divine Mind shows me how to use them wisely for the good of all. I am prospered in all my affairs and I thank the source of all Good.

By using a treatment, such as the above, we learn to follow the guidance of Divine Mind in handling our own gifts and abilities. We are led to the right sources, opportunities and our way is prospered. The wisdom of the Infinite is always available, but it is up to us to put it to use. This is accomplished by dwelling upon truth, goodness, kindness, mercy and understanding. Appreciation for spiritual values puts at our disposal the boundless wealth of God.

CHAPTER 8

Healing Power of God

"Bless the Lord, O my soul: and all that is within me, bless his holy name."
"Bless the Lord, O my soul, and forget not all his benefits:
"Who forgiveth all thine iniquities, who healeth all thy diseases."

Psalm 103:1-3

Health is important to everyone. The word means "wholeness" and man should be whole in mind, soul and body; however he has believed that sin, sickness, and disease are his lot; and also believed that when he reaches a certain age he is no longer useful. Jesus reversed this trend of thinking. He boldly declared: "I am come that they might have life, and that they might have it more abundantly." John 10:10.

Man has forgotten that he was created a spiritual being and it is the spiritual side of his nature that he should nurture to overcome the age-old beliefs in sin, sickness, disease and poverty. Many of these erroneous beliefs are deeply imbedded in the subconscious mind, in fact, he may not always be aware that they exist. Once he begins to watch his thinking and observes the kind of thoughts that rise to the surface of consciousness, he discovers that he has been holding on to much that needs to be eliminated.

49

Divine Mind can heal anywhere, any place, at any time. Mind is omnipresent and works to bring forth a perfect pattern whenever the individual is receptive to its benign influence.

One cool fall evening I went to the corner drug store to purchase a few items. There was no urgent need for the things I intended to purchase and had I looked at the clock I would not have started out. The drug store's closing hour was nine o'clock and when I arrived it was closed. I wondered why I had not looked at the clock before leaving home, but I soon learned that,

"God moves in a mysterious way,
his wonders to perform." (*William Cowper*)

Just as I started to turn away a friend approached me and said: "I am so glad to see you," and then I noticed that she had been crying. Her husband had died a few months before and I thought perhaps she had taken a walk to help assuage her grief. I asked her if there was anything I could do for her.

Emma answered, "I am very ill, suffering from shortness of breath. I ache all over and my throat is raw and sore. I tried to call the family physician but he is out of town, then I decided to pull myself together and go to church. I wanted to light a candle and pray, but the church was closed when I got there. Then I thought I would go to the drug store and see if the druggist could suggest something that would help me. Now, as you can see, the drug store is closed, and I don't know what to do," and the tears started to flow again.

I said to her, "Emma, my way of praying may be different from yours, but I do not think it makes any difference to God. Perhaps if we walk to the side of the building and

50

pray together you will feel better. I believe that God can heal anyone, any place, anywhere and at any time."

She said she would be most grateful for any assistance I might give her, and so we moved to the side of the building. She gripped my hand very tightly and I sensed that she wanted help very much. I began to treat for wholeness and suddenly a very peaceful feeling descended upon me. I was no longer conscious of the cool, sharp evening air, or even the presence of Emma. I seemed to be enveloped in a wonderful, warm glow of some kind. I was conscious of speaking words of healing, but nothing more. Suddenly I had the assurance within me that the healing had taken place and I became aware of Emma saying: "I feel better now, I can go home." I knew she was healed.

Bright and early the next morning Emma telephoned that she had slept soundly; her aches and pains were all gone and her throat was healed. She was a nurse and told me that it was the first time in her life she had ever experienced an instantaneous healing. Her desire for healing was so intense, her faith so strong at that particular time, that she was completely receptive to the healing flow of Divine Love within her as it washed away all aches and pains and restored her to wholeness.

In his fine book . . . *The Science of Successful Living* Raymond Charles Barker says: "In you the power of accomplishment is unlimited. But it must have free and open channels through which to work. You alone can clog or clear the channels of consciousness." Emma had cleared the channels of her consciousness and when this was accomplished she was healed.

It is wonderful to know that there is a power that takes care of us, when we are in difficulty. It is a blessing to know

* Dr. Raymond Charles Barker is minister of the First Church of Religious Science, New York City.

that God, the all-knowing Mind is ever available and we can call upon it to help us.

I spent a vacation one time, with my friend, the Reverend Millie Leslie, at a southern seashore resort. The weather was pleasant and many hours were spent watching the ocean, the fishing vessels as they started out early in the morning, and the people who fished from the piers. Terns and sandpipers came playfully along the beach and sea gulls flew overhead. Porpoises and fish popped up and down as they swam along. During the day the ocean was usually calm and the lapping of the waves against the shore was soothing and restful, but when the tides came in it was awesome to watch the waters become turbulent. Far in the distance the white caps appeared and the breakers seemed to gain momentum as they moved toward and crashed against the shore with a loud thud, bringing the water farther inward, and then receding again.

As I watched and listened to the waves, I thought of the great intelligence that had formed the waters and planned the rhythm and movement of the waves. With all its tremendous power, the ocean was still held in bounds by the Divine Mind, that had set a firmament in the midst of the waters, and divided the waters from the waters.

Little did I realize as I pondered these things that the same evening I would have an opportunity of seeing the healing, saving power of the Infinite at work in a wonderful way. We had taken a walk and enjoyed the evening breeze when we noticed considerable activity on the ocean. Numerous ships with search lights on had converged on an area and lighted up the ocean, while planes were flying overhead. As the lights from the ships and planes played upon the Atlantic ocean a number of people gathered along the beach to watch this extraordinary sight. We were told that a plane

---

* The Reverend Millie Leslie is minister of the Unity Temple of Truth, Cincinnati, Ohio.

had radioed for help and the ships and other planes had rushed to the rescue. The airman was found alive and flown to his base. Gradually the planes and ships vanished and the darkness of the night took over. It was truly wonderful to consider that so much effort had been put forth to save a life. The healing power works in many ways and every soul is important to God.

The Christ consciousness is truly our Hope of Glory and when we heed it and give it free rein the results are often beyond our expectations. Where there is a strong desire to live, even in the face of disastrous circumstances, man can be healed.

A good neighbor stopped me as I was entering the church one morning and requested me to call on a family that lived a few doors from her. The husband had been critically in- jured in an automobile accident and was not expected to live. The wife had asked the neighbor to get in touch with me. As I walked into the room the man was having great difficulty breathing, and the wife whispered that he was not expected to live throughout the day. I began to treat. It seemed to me that I could only think of Life. It was the word that was paramount. "Declare *Life,* see him as a son of life and light" was the inner message. When human thinking was finally quieted and the inner stillness took over it seemed to me that the man was breathing easier.

Within a week I was asked to call again and was told he was improving. A few weeks later he sat up for a little while each day and gradually he gained enough strength to walk. Neighbors and friends were astounded at his recovery. It so happened that the man and his wife were very coopera- tive. They held on to the idea of life, even though there were times when he seemed to be losing ground, and he came through.

In this man's healing one could really see faith in action. What is faith? It isn't something you can put your finger on and say: "Here it is" but you can see it in action. It is something that can be felt within and that the mind can take hold of. Faith is a firm belief in something, an unshakable trust in a Power, in God, that everything will work out in the right way. Faith is a strong, definite expectation, that despite appearances to the contrary good must ultimately prevail. It is confidence in Divine Mind that it is forever working for the well-being of the individual.

Faith is important in all healing. Faith means trust and it helps a man to hold on, to expect good, in the face of many odds. The man who has faith in God has composure; something within that is reassuring, and it gives him the patience to let things work out as they should. Faith is not passive; it is a mighty, active power that produces results. The man who has faith in Divine Mind does not waste his time and thinking on things that are useless and unproductive. He has confidence in his own God-given ability not to allow others to discourage or dissuade him from his course. There may be times when doubts creep in, but the persevering individual centers all his attention on his goal and expects the demonstration to follow: This requires,

1. Perseverance in face of dismal appearances
2. Composure
3. Patience
4. Continual spiritual treatment
5. Faith that the outcome will be good.

Thomas à Kempis said: "If thou trust in the Lord, strength will be given thee from heaven, and the world and the flesh will be made subject to thy sway."

In the thirteenth chapter of Matthew it is related that when Jesus returned to his own country and taught in the synagogue, people were astonished, but he was not able to do mighty healing works there because of their unbelief. To the people of his own country he was one of them and they would not believe that he could help them. They were not willing to believe that faith is an invisible power and its constructive use brings right results. Had Jesus come from afar and given the same message to his people they might have believed, as Thomas Campbell wrote:

"'Tis distance lends enchantment to the view,
And robes the mountain in its azure hue."

The fact that Jesus was not accepted among his people did not lessen his faith in his own ability nor in God. When he went to the coasts of Tyre and Sidon he was again able to continue his healing work, because people believed in him and in God's power to heal. They brought those who were lame, blind, dumb, maimed, and he healed them. He did not take credit for the healings but stated humbly, "the Father that dwelleth in me, he doeth the works" John 14:10. A deeply implanted faith becomes the agency through which the God mind can accomplish its purpose. God never forsakes his children. There is an inner light, the Christ light, which takes us from darkness and despair into the light and the day dawns.

I have faith in the power of God within me to heal every inharmonious condition. My faith is strong and unshakable. I am free from doubt and fear. I praise the power of Divine Mind for the wonderful way in which it takes care of me.

CHAPTER 9

Life and Love

Life is. We know that it exists, it is something we cannot do without and yet we really do not know what it is. All physical form contains life, whether it is man, animal, insect, plant or planet. "See, I have set before thee this day life and good. . . ." Deut. 35:15. The seasons come and go with regularity, they merge into one another and are proof that there is a mighty mind at work in the universe.

Joseph W. Hoffman* writes: "Life is both a miracle and a mystery. No scientist can tell what it is or from where it comes or goes. No one can tell at what point a man's body dies. There is a legal definition of death, a medical definition, and a biological one. Some day soon biologists will 'create' life in a test tube but, like Dr. Frankenstein building his monster from parts of dead bodies, they will be merely arranging matter and life will remain still a miracle. Life is both a miracle and a mystery and we call that mystery and miracle God."

Life is the great unexplainable something in the Universe but it is love working with life that performs the miracles in people's lives. We find this description of love in 1 Corin-

---

* Mr. Joseph W. Hoffman is a science teacher in the Cincinnati schools, a Religious Science practitioner, and a teacher in the First Church of Religious Science. The quotation in this chapter is from an unpublished manuscript.

thians 13:47; "Love is patient and kind, love is not jealous or boastful; it is not arrogant or rude. Love does not insist on its own way; it is not irritable or resentful; it does not rejoice at wrong, but rejoices in the right. Love bears all things, believes all things, hopes all things, endures all things."

A miracle is an event or effect in the physical world which cannot be explained. It seems to defy all known laws and yet in a real sense there can be no deviation from law. What we consider a miracle is the acceleration of the tempo of the individual mind in merging with the universal mind, and through this speeded up movement the inner and outer are unified. When what seems to be a miracle happens in a person's life, you can be sure that a great amount of mental and spiritual treatment has taken place for a long time. Gradually the spiritual treatment is able to penetrate the deeper layers of the subconscious and eliminate fears and wrong thinking. When the inner work is accomplished the demonstration takes place.

There are many things which we cannot explain at present but as we learn more about the way in which the mind works, they will be understood. Many things that were considered magical in the past can now be satisfactorily explained as the outworking of a mental law.

Love is non-resistant. It does not fight to get its way. If you are slandered or someone tries to take what is yours, the first tendency is to retaliate. If you can resist this impulse and refrain from returning evil for evil you have taken the first step. The second step is far more difficult, but you should return good for evil. You can forgive and pray for the offender. These two steps clear the consciousness of resentment and this is practising true non-resistance.

Water is a non-resistant force. It does not worry about obstacles but flows around them and wears them away by constantly pouring itself upon them. Love is like that. It is constantly pouring itself into all living things. It disregards human weaknesses; it is not revengeful, but through patience eventually overcomes all hard conditions. When love has full sway miracles happen.

A woman who owned a grocery store for many years decided to sell it. She was an honest person and kind to every one. At the time she sold the store she was certain that all bills had been paid, but to her great surprise her attorney told her that the attorney for the buyer had dis- covered an uncancelled lien, showing that she owed the former owner five hundred dollars. She was sure that she had paid the debt, but the mortgage for five hundred dollars had never been cancelled at the court house where it was recorded.

She got in touch with me and we treated for evidence to prove that the mortgage had been paid. Later that after- noon she telephoned and said after the turmoil and worry subsided and she had been able to quiet her thinking, she remembered that she had saved her cancelled checks for years and intended to go through them. An hour later I re- ceived a joyous call, the cancelled check for five hundred dollars had been found, and within a few days the legal technicalities were settled, the record was cleared and she received the full purchase price for her store. Her goodness was a bulwark in the time of difficulty.

Many homes would be happier if at least one member of the household would remember that "love bears all things." Late one afternoon while I was working alone in the church the telephone rang and a man said, "I want to talk to the minister." I told him that I was the minister and asked if I could help him. Then he answered rather dejectly, "Oh— You are a woman." Then a long silence ensued. He was debating whether or not he wanted to talk with me and I waited until he made up his mind.

Finally he said, "Well, maybe you can help me. I am

having trouble with my wife—she wants to leave me." I suggested that they come in together and we could discuss the problem and treat for a way out of the difficulty, but he was in no mood for that. His reply was, "No, I'm sending my wife, she is the one who needs help," and then he hung up. I thought that ended the matter but a few days later I received a call from his wife, asking for an appointment.

She was a lovely person with a nice friendly manner. She said that she had no intention of leaving her husband but they had been quarreling over finances. They lived in a small town and the plant where her husband had worked for many years had closed its doors. He had made a valiant effort to get a job but had been rejected everywhere because of his age. As we turned to Divine Mind for guidance it seemed advisable for the wife to seek employment to tide the family over the critical financial period. Shortly thereafter she found employment in a neighboring town and was able to commute to and from work, and this eased the financial tensions. In the meantime the husband took whatever odd jobs he was able to get. Finally they saved enough money to purchase a small truck and he eventually worked up a lucrative business hauling merchandise and equipment for business houses.

After the financial problem was solved the husband said he wanted to meet the woman minister. They came to church one Sunday morning and after the service as he shook hands with me he said he guessed he changed his mind about women preachers. In his book they were all right.

Love is not demanding. It frees people to live their own lives and the power of love works in the animal world as well. Browne Landone, an early New Thought teacher was given a surly dog. He treated every day for the dog to display love but the dog's disposition did not improve. In fact it snarled and growled and showed its teeth every time he came near it. Then he decided to give the dog freedom. He no longer treated for the dog to change its disposition but treated himself that he would always think of the dog in a loving way. That worked the miracle. Within a short time the dog began to show a real affection for Mr. Landone and barked joyously whenever he came into the house.

One of the greatest miracles and blessings in life is to be free from a sense of guilt, or frustration, or to be free from illness or disease. If you need money and are burdened with debts and the mailman brings a check to pay them, your frustration vanishes. The burden has been lifted, and that is exactly what love does.

Love casts its bread on the waters of life freely. It is not concerned as to how it is returned, or what sources God uses. It gives of itself when and where it is needed. Love accepts as graciously as it gives. Some people do not prosper because of their reluctance to receive. If you want other people to accept your love, gifts, and friendship, then you must be willing to accept what is sent to you in the spirit of divine love.

Appreciation, a word of thanks to God is as important as a word of thanks to someone who has been kind to you. Your gratitude and love do not change God, but you are changed. God is Love. Trust and believe in the power of Divine Mind: "for with God all things are possible." Mark 10:27.